Workbook for Presentation Skills

— BASIC —

[Revised Edition]

実践プレゼンテーション・ワークブック
入門編（二訂版）

NAKAYAMA, Tomokazu
SCHNICKEL, Jacob
BULACH, Juergen

Asahi Press

Workbook for Presentation Skills —Basic— [Revised Edition]

Copyright © 2024 by Asahi Press

Preface

This workbook has been made especially to help you improve your presentation skills in English as well as to support you in becoming a more confident and competent English user, targeting the B1 level on the CEFR. This means that completing all the tasks in this textbook will not only improve your presentation skills but will also push you to be a more advanced user of English.

There are two reasons we chose to call this a workbook rather than a textbook. One is that half of the book is blank so that you, the learner, can fill in the blanks and make your *own book*. The second reason is that this book will really make you work to complete each task.

This workbook repeats the same procedure in each unit: Make an Outline, Make a Script, Make a Poster, and Rehearse. The reason for this repetition is that gaining the skills to make a presentation is not a simple process, especially for Japanese learners, whose native language is totally different from English and who also have different ways of presenting thoughts. We need to repeat the same procedure to become accustomed to giving presentations in English in terms of both language choice and organization of thought.

We are quite confident that you will learn efficient presentation skills if you complete all the tasks in this workbook. We hope you enjoy the process.

CONTENTS

Unit 0 What is a Presentation? 1
    DAY 1: Practice the Sample Presentation 1

Unit 1 Describing Your Hometown 5
    DAY 2: Make an Outline 6
    DAY 3: Write a Presentation Script and Make a Poster 9
    DAY 4: Rehearse Presentation 21

Rubric I 22

Unit 2 Which Hamburger Shop Do You Like the Best? 23
    DAY 5: Read an Article and Make an Outline 24
    DAY 6: Write a Presentation Script and Make a Poster 34
    DAY 7: Rehearse Presentation 46

Unit 3 Fashion: Which Apparel Brand Do You Prefer? 47
    DAY 8: Read an Article and Make an Outline 48
    DAY 9: Write a Presentation Script and Make a Poster 60
    DAY 10: Rehearse Presentation 65

Unit 4 Product Development 66
    DAY 11: Write a Product Proposal and Make an Outline 66
    DAY 12: Write a Presentation Script and Make a Poster 72
    DAY 13: Rehearse Presentation 77

Rubric II 78

Unit 5 Is Study Abroad Necessary? 79
    DAY 14: Read an Article and Make an Outline 79
    DAY 15: Write a Presentation Script and Make a Poster 88
    DAY 16: Rehearse Presentation 93

Rubrics III 94

Appendix 95

Vocabulary 96

For Students

After you go through this workbook, you will be better able to

1. use English without hesitation.
2. plan and make a basic English presentation.
3. explain your ideas more clearly.

How will you be able to achieve these goals?

1. **Learning Begins with Imitation**

   In each unit, there is a model presentation script provided to help you organize your own script. You may make necessary changes to the model phrases or sentences to suit your purpose. By repeating this process, you can expand your repertoire of ways to express your thoughts.

2. **Practice Makes Perfect**

   You will be asked to do the same type of tasks twice: the first time with instructions, the second time on your own so that you can learn the structures and necessary phrases better. You will also be asked to do some tasks at least 5 times in total so that you can learn them thoroughly.

3. **Rubrics**

   You will be provided rubrics and be asked to self-evaluate to see your own progress.

本書で学ばれる皆さんへ

このテキストで学ぶと

---

1. 躊躇なく英語が使えるようになります。

2. 英語による基本的なプレゼンテーションを作り行うことができます。

3. 自分の考えをもっとわかりやすく表現できるようになります。

本書では以上の３つの目標が達成できるように、以下の３つの手法を取り入れています。

1. 学習は模倣から始まる。

　それぞれのユニットには、台本作成の助けとなるように、モデルの台本が用意されています。必要に応じて、モデルにあるフレーズや文をどんどん使って、自分自身の考えを表現してください。

2. 習うより慣れろ！

　本書は、最終的にプレゼンテーションの全てを台本なしで行えるように、同じ内容を繰り返し学習できるよう工夫がされています。Unit 1 を終えるまでには、Introduction を、Unit 3 を終えるまでには、Body を、そして Unit 5 を終えるまでには、全てのプレゼンテーションを台本なしで、こなすことを目標としてください。

3. ルーブリック (Rubrics)

　２ユニットが終わるごとに、ルーブリックが用意されています。本書での学習を終えるときには、全ての項目が、Level 3 に到達できるように頑張ってください。

DAY 1

Learn from the Sample Presentation

Ⓐ Practice the Sample Presentation

The following is a very concrete sample of a presentation. Practice with your partner.

<本ユニットの課題>
このユニットでは、「食べ物」に関する簡単なプレゼンテーション例を使って、プレゼンテーションの基礎を
理解します。

(INTRODUCTION)

Did you know a banana is a fruit? Have you imagined that a lettuce is a vegetable? Did you also know that chicken is a kind of meat? Hi, my name is Utako Shimoda. I am a student at JW University. Today, I will talk about food. Hopefully by the end of presentation, you will better understand food. I will focus on fruit, vegetables and meat.

(Body)

I would like to begin by talking about fruits. A banana is a fruit. Moreover, a strawberry is a fruit, too. Finally, an orange is a fruit. So a banana, a strawberry and an orange are kinds of fruit.

I've talked about fruits. But what about vegetables? Next, I would like to talk about vegetables. First, broccoli is a vegetable. Lettuce is a vegetable, too. Finally, a carrot is a vegetable. So broccoli, lettuce and carrots are kinds of vegetables.

I've finished talking about vegetables. But what about meat? Finally I would like to talk about meat. First, pork is a kind of meat. Second, beef is a kind of meat. Finally, chicken is a kind of meat. So pork, beef and chicken are different kinds of meat.

(Conclusion)

Let me summarize the points of today's presentation. I talked about food today. First, I talked about fruit. I told you that a banana, a strawberry and an orange are fruits. Second, I talked about vegetables. I told you that broccoli, lettuce and carrots are vegetables. Finally, I talked about meat. I told you that pork, beef and chicken are kinds of meat. I hope you have a better understanding of food and that you'll be more interested in what you eat. Thank you for listening. Do you have any questions?

DAY 1

Ⓑ Make an outline from the sample.

<ポイント：サンプルからアウトラインを起こしてみましょう。>

1. INTRODUCTION

A. Hook <ポイント：聞き手を引きつけるための投げかけ>
B. Self-introduction
C. Purpose statement <ポイント：プレゼンテーションの目的>
D. Objective statement <ポイント：目標　このプレゼンテーションを聞いた後、聞き手にどうしてほしいのかの記述>

2. BODY <ポイント：常に3つ以上のトピックが必要です。>

A. Topic 1: Fruit

Topic sentence
Supporting detail 1
Supporting detail 2
Supporting detail 3
Benefit <ポイント：Benefit には、それぞれのトピックの詳細のまとめを記述します>

B. Topic 2

Topic sentence	
Supporting detail 1	
Supporting detail 2	
Supporting detail 3	
Benefit	

C. Topic 3

Topic sentence	
Supporting detail 1	
Supporting detail 2	
Supporting detail 3	
Benefit	

DAY 1

3. CONCLUSION <ポイント：結論では「目的」、「トピックのまとめ」および「目標」を繰り返し、聞き手にあなたのプレゼンテーションを印象付けます。>

A. Purpose statement
B. Topic sentence 1 and Benefit（Benefit を忘れずに）
C. Topic sentence 2 and Benefit（Benefit を忘れずに）
D. Topic sentence 3 and Benefit（Benefit を忘れずに）
E. Final remark (Objective statement)

Unit 1 Describing Your Hometown

TASK You are a student at JW University. You have been assigned to be hometown ambassador by your local tourist office and asked to give presentations in English to travel agencies overseas to attract tourists to your hometown.

＜本ユニットの課題＞
あなたは JW 大学の学生です。この度地元の観光協会から町の観光大使に選ばれました。海外からの旅行者を呼び寄せるために、外国の旅行代理店に向けて英語でプレゼンテーションをしてください。

The local tourist office has asked you to include the following *three topics* in your presentation.

---

1. **A brief overview of your hometown**
   (ex. Location, population, climate and so on)

2. **Three to four main attractions in your hometown**
   (ex. Cherry blossom viewing, fishing and so on)

3. **Accommodations (Hotels)**

DAY 2
Make an Outline

The official at your local tourist office asks for the outline of your presentation. Write your outline using the following format:

1. INTRODUCTION

    A. Hook <ポイント：聞き手を引きつけるための投げかけ>

    _____

    B. Self-introduction

    _____

    C. Purpose statement <ポイント：プレゼンテーションの目的>

    _____

    D. Objective statement <ポイント：目標　このプレゼンテーションを聞いた後、聞き手にどうしてほしいのかの記述>

    _____

2. A brief overview of your hometown

    A. Location

    How far is it from Tokyo?

    _____

    How long does it take to get there from Tokyo?

    _____

    B. Population

    What is the population of your hometown?

    _____

    C. Climate

    What is the average temperature in spring?

    _____

    What is the average temperature in summer?

    _____

What is the average temperature in fall?

_____

What is the average temperature in winter?

_____

D. Benefit

Why is your hometown attractive in terms of location?

_____

3. Main attractions in your hometown

A. Spring

What kinds of events, activities or attractions can tourists enjoy in spring?

_____

B. Summer

What kinds of events, activities or attractions can tourists enjoy in summer?

_____

C. Fall

What kinds of events, activities or attractions can tourists enjoy in fall?

_____

D. Winter

What kinds of events, activities or attractions can tourists enjoy in winter?

_____

E. Benefit

Why is your hometown attractive in terms of events, activities and/or attractions?

_____

DAY 2

4. Accommodations in your hometown

A. Expensive hotels
What is the cost of an expensive hotel?

_____

B. Medium priced hotels
What is the cost of a medium priced hotel?

_____

C. Reasonable hotels
What is the cost of a reasonable hotel?

_____

D. Benefits
Why is your hometown attractive in terms of accommodations?

_____

5. Conclusion <ポイント：結論では、以下の情報を繰り返して聞き手に伝えます。>

A. Purpose statement

_____

B. Topic 1 and Benefit（Benefit を忘れずに）

_____

C. Topic 2 and Benefit（Benefit を忘れずに）

_____

D. Topic 3 and Benefit（Benefit を忘れずに）

_____

E. Final remark (Objective statement)

_____

DAY 3
Write a Presentation Script and Make a Poster

TASK You've received approval from the tourist office. Now write a script for your presentation and make a presentation poster.

<課題：アウトラインを使って、台本とポスターを作りましょう。>

A Confirm Structure of Presentation

Any presentation consists of three sections (INTRODUCTION, BODY and CONCLUSION). Each section has a specific role that helps listeners clearly understand your presentation. Skipping any of these sections will confuse listeners.

<**ポイント**：プレゼンテーションは、1. イントロダクション（INTRODUCTION） 2. 本論（BODY） 3. 結論（CONCLUSION）の3つの構成から成り立っています。これら3つはそれぞれ重要な役割を持っており、どの部分が欠けてもプレゼンテーションにはなりません。>

1. INTRODUCTION

A. **Introduction of yourself** <自己紹介>

B. **Purpose of your presentation** <目的>
なぜプレゼンテーションを行うのかを述べる

Ex. The purpose of this presentation is to tell you three unique features of Hachikuni.

C. **Objective of your presentation:** <目標>
聞き手にこのプレゼンテーションを聞き終わったらどうしてほしいかを述べる。

Ex. Hopefully by the end of this presentation, you will be interested in this wonderful city, Hachikuni.

DAY 3

2. BODY (At least 3 Topics)

A. Topic 1 Topic sentence
    a. Supporting detail 1
    b. Supporting detail 2
    c. Supporting detail 3
    d. Benefit

B. Topic 2 Topic sentence
    a. Supporting detail 1
    b. Supporting detail 2
    c. Supporting detail 3
    d. Benefit

C. Topic 3 Topic sentence
    a. Supporting detail 1
    b. Supporting detail 2
    c. Supporting detail 3
    d. Benefit

* Benefit is a statement that summarizes the good points for the listener. There is a benefit statement at the end of each topic.

＜ポイント：Benefit には、それぞれのトピックの詳細から、聞き手にとってどんな利点があるのかを記述します。＞

3. CONCLUSION

A. Purpose statement repeated

B. Topic 1 and Benefit

C. Topic 2 and Benefit

D. Topic 3 and Benefit

E. Objective statement repeated

TENSE use in each section

FUTURE Tense is used in the INTRODUCTION section.
＜ポイント：イントロダクションでは、未来形が多く使われます。＞

・ Today, I'm going to talk about…

・ I will cover three points today…

FUTURE and/or PRESENT Tense is / are used in the BODY section.
＜ポイント：本論では未来形あるいは、現在形が多く使われます。＞

・ As you can see…

・ This means that…

PAST TENSE and/or PRESENT PERFECT is/are used in the CONCLUSION section.
＜ポイント：結論では過去形あるいは完了形が多く使われます。＞

・ Today, I talked about…

・ I explained…

・ I have shown that…

DAY 3

B **Write a Script of Your Presentation.**

You will write a script for your presentation. The sample formats are provided for your reference.

Your Introduction

Sample Introduction

Did you know that we can ski in Hachikuni?

Hi. Thank you so much for giving me an opportunity to make a presentation on Hachikuni. My name is Utako Shimoda. I am a student at JW University. The purpose of today's presentation is to present three unique features of Hachikuni. Hopefully, by the end of this presentation, you will be interested in Hachikuni and bring many tourists to this wonderful city.

Hook

Purpose Statement

Objective Statement

DAY 3

Your Body

Sample Body

First, I would like to talk about the location and the climate of my town. Hachikuni is located about 70 kilometers northwest of Tokyo. We have a population of 150,000. The average temperature in spring is 15 degrees Celsius; in summer, it is 28 degrees in fall; it is 20 degrees; and in winter it is 10 degrees. Hachikuni is situated in the suburbs of Tokyo and has a mild climate.

Second, I would like to talk about some of the main attractions in Hachikuni. We can do cherry blossom viewing in spring. We can enjoy swimming at Hachikuni Land, an amusement park, in summer. We can enjoy looking at beautiful autumn leaves in fall. And in winter, we can ski at Mt. Hachikuni. In Hachikuni we can enjoy a variety of activities all year around.

Third, I would like to talk about accommodations in Hachikuni. An expensive hotel is ABC Hotel at 8,000 yen per night. A medium priced hotel is DEF Hotel at 5,000 yen per night. An inexpensive hotel is GHI Hotel at 4,000 yen per night. All of them are clean and comfortable. People can choose suitable hotels according to their needs.

Topic sentence

Benefit statement

DAY 3

Your Conclusion

Sample Conclusion

In conclusion, today I talked about three unique features of Hachikuni. First, I talked about location. It is located about 70 km northwest of Tokyo. Second, I talked about its main attractions. I told you that we can enjoy various activities throughout the year. Third, I talked about accommodations in Hachikuni. I told you that people can choose suitable hotels according to their needs. Now you know that Hachikuni can entertain people of all ages with varying interests all year long. Hopefully, you will remember Hachikuni and bring many tourists to this wonderful city in Japan. Thank you for listening. Do you have any questions?

Benefits should be repeated.

DAY 3

Check Your Script

1. Does your script have five paragraphs?

    YES   NO

2. Is your purpose statement included in the INTRODUCTION?

    YES   NO

3. Is your objective statement included in the INTRODUCTION?

    YES   NO

4. Does each BODY paragraph have three supporting details?

    YES   NO

5. Does each BODY paragraph have a benefit statement?

    YES   NO

6. Does the CONCLUSION paragraph have three topic sentences and 3 benefits?

    YES   NO

7. Does the CONCLUSION paragraph have an objective statement?

    YES   NO

8. Did you use the past tense or present perfect in the CONCLUSION paragraph?

    YES   NO

C Make a Poster

A clear and interesting presentation poster not only attracts listeners but also promotes a better understanding of your message. Think about what kind of information should be included in your poster to make your presentation more attractive.

DAY 3

This is a sample presentation poster.

Hachikuni: A Fantastic Place to Visit

Utako Shimoda
JW University

Purpose: To introduce three unique features of Hachikuni

1. Location and Climate

Location: 70 km from Tokyo

Population: 150,000

Average Temperature by Season in Hachikuni

Spring	Summer	Fall	Winter
15 ℃	28 ℃	20 ℃	10℃

2. Main Attractions

Cherry Blossom Viewing

Swimming

Autumn Leaves

Skiing

3. Accommodations

ABC Hotel

8000 yen

DEF Hotel

5000 yen

GHI Hotel

4000 yen

Conclusion

Hachikuni can entertain people of all ages with varying interests throughout the year.

DAY 4
Rehearse Presentation

TASK   You will give your presentation tomorrow. Now practice your presentation with your friends.

Practice makes perfect. Find a partner and practice your presentation. Ask your partners to evaluate your presentation on the following points, rating each from 1 to 5.

1. **The speaker's voice was loud enough to hear.**

   1   2   3   4   5

   ↑ strongly disagree   ↑ strongly agree

2. **The delivery speed was appropriate.**

   1   2   3   4   5

3. **The speaker used the poster effectively.**

   1   2   3   4   5

4. **The speaker looked at the audience.**

   1   2   3   4   5

5. **You were interested in this presentation.**

   1   2   3   4   5

What questions would you like to ask the speaker?

_____

_____

_____

Final Task

Record your script into your cellphone and practice parallel reading until you can say all the words without looking at your script.

DAY 4

Self-evaluation Rubric I

以下の表中の①〜③について、今の自分がどのレベルにいるか、それぞれあてはまるセルにチェックをしましょう。

	Level 1	Level 2	Level 3
① **Presentation Structure**	I can write an outline if I use this book. ＿＿＿	I can write an outline without this book. ＿＿＿	I can explain how to make an outline to my friends. ＿＿＿
② **Presentation Script**	I can write a script if I have this book. ＿＿＿	I can write a script without this book. ＿＿＿	I can explain how to write a script to my friends. ＿＿＿
③ **Presentation**	I can make a presentation if I have a script. ＿＿＿	I can make a presentation without a script. ＿＿＿	I can make an effective presentation using a poster. ＿＿＿

Unit 2

Which Hamburger Shop Do You Like the Best?

TASK You need to give a presentation about the food industry in your next economics class. You and one of your classmates decided to compare JN Burger and Traditional Burger with one of your classmates. Please compare the two hamburger shops and prepare a presentation on them.

＜本ユニットの課題＞

次の経済学の授業で、食品産業についてのプレゼンテーションをしなくてはいけません。あなたは、クラスメイトと一緒に JN Burger と Traditional Burger を比較することにしました。2つのハンバーガーショップを比較してプレゼンテーションを行ってください。

JN Burger

Traditional Burger

DAY 5
Read an Article and Make an Outline

🅐 Read the Website

You found the following information on the hamburger shops' websites. Please read the websites. Student A will read about JN Burger, and Student B will read about Traditional Burger.

＜課題：パートナーのどちらか一方が JN Burger のホームページを読み、もう一方が Traditional Burger のホームページを読みましょう＞

JN Burger

Message from the President

Thank you so much for your patronage of JN Burger. We have been serving customers healthy and delicious food since our first store opened in 1975. Under our motto, "Sharing a wonderful and rich life with customers," we have been trying to create not only wholesome, tasty food but also a unique dining experience. Beginning with our Curry Burger, we have introduced about 30 unique burgers to satisfy various customers from children to the elderly. We will never stop challenging ourselves to exceed our customers' expectations.

We put a great deal of effort into serving fresh meals to our customers. To achieve this, eighty percent of our stores are equipped with their own onsite vegetable production facilities. We also continue to apply an "after-order" cooking system, for which we start to cook after we have taken an order from a customer.

We will continue making efforts to maintain our customers' trust. We are looking forward to serving you soon.

M. Tajima
President of JN burger

Corporate Profile

Company Name	JN Burger. Inc
Head Office	1-1-49, Higashi, Shibuya-ku, Tokyo, Japan
Date of Establishment	August 8, 1975
Capital Stock	3.5 billion yen (As of April 2017)

End of Fiscal Year	March 31
Number of Employees	3,250 (As of April 2023)
Description of Business	Operations of JN Burger Shops
Numbers of Stores	Japan: 250 China: 80, Korea: 60, Indonesia: 45, Malaysia: 45, US: 40, UK: 35, Germany: 10 (Total: 565)

History of JN Burger Inc.

1975   First store opened in Ginza

1980   15th store opened in Hokkaido

1985   "After order" system introduced in all the stores

1991   100th store opened in Okinawa

1998   Curry Burger was introduced

2001   First stores in the US and the UK opened

2008   Onsite vegetable facilities introduced

2010   First store opened in China

2023   565th store opened in Malaysia

Menu		Side Orders	
Burger + 300 yen = Set Menu		**Fries**	
(Set Menu = Burger + French Fries + Drink)		French Fries S	150 yen
		M	200 yen
Hamburgers		L	250 yen
Summer Special	380 yen	Onion Rings	200 yen
Curry Burger	350 yen		
Soba Burger	300 yen	**Salad**	
Regular Burger	150 yen	Special Salad	300 yen
Cheeseburger	200 yen		
		Soup	
Drinks		Corn Soup	150 yen
Cola	150 yen	Vegetable Soup	200 yen
Orange Juice	200 yen		
Vegetable Juice	200 yen	**Dessert**	
		Vanilla Ice Cream	100 yen

DAY 5

Traditional Burger

Message from the President

Thank you so much for your patronage of Traditional Burger. Since our first store opened in 1950, under the motto, "Keep Tradition, Make History," we have been serving our original 100% beef patty hamburger as it was first made in a small U.S. town called Hamburg. Since we served our first customer, we have maintained the traditional way of cooking beef patties. To ensure the quality of our traditional burgers, we ship our original patties, charcoal, and buns from our own factories in the U.S. by air to locations all over the world. Furthermore, we provide 30 day training to franchise owners to ensure the same quality of our traditional burgers. We have been working hard to serve customers with the best ingredients and the same quality of hamburgers since we opened our first store.

We will continue to make efforts to gain trust from our customers. We are looking forward to serving you soon.

J. Bulach
President of Traditional Burger Inc.

Corporate Profile

Company Name	Traditional Burger. Inc.
Head Office	123rd St., Hamburg, WV, U.S.
Date of Establishment	July 8, 1950
Capital Stock	35 million dollars (As of April 2023)
End of Fiscal Year	October 1
Number of Employees	3,250 (As of April 2023)
Description of Business	Operations of Traditional Burger Shops
Numbers of Stores	U.S.: 250 UK: 85 Germany: 80 Japan: 35 Korea: 35 Indonesia: 35 Malaysia: 35 China: 10 (Total: 565)

History of Traditional Burger Inc.

1950 First store opened in Hamburg

1965 15th store opened in Hawaii

1970 First store opened in the UK

1975 100th store opened in Tokyo

1980 Started shipping materials by air

2001 First store in Korea opened

2008 First store opened in Indonesia

2010 First store opened in China

2023 565th store opened in Indonesia

Menu	Side Orders	
Burger + 400 yen = Set Menu	**Fries**	
(Set Menu = Burger + French Fries + Drink)	French Fries S	150 yen
	M	200 yen
Hamburgers	L	250 yen
Single Traditional Burger 380 yen		
Double Traditional Burger 420 yen	**Dessert**	
Triple Traditional Burger 440 yen	Vanilla Ice Cream	150 yen
*Single= 1 patty, Double= 2 patties, Triple = 3 patties		
Drinks		
Cola 150 yen		
Root Beer 150 yen		
Orange Juice 200 yen		

DAY 5

B Make an Outline

You need to show your outline to your supervisor. Find a partner. Student A will fill in the blanks about JN Burger. Student B will fill in the blanks about Traditional Burger. Once finished, ask questions to each other in English to get the missing information, and complete the outline. Then decide which hamburger shop you want to recommend.

＜課題：パートナーの一方が、JN Burger の空欄に、もう一方が Traditional Burger の空欄に必要な情報を書きましょう。書き終わったらお互いに英語で質問をして、相手の持っている情報を書き入れましょう。それからどちらのハンバーガーショップを宣伝するか決めて、下の Objective statement の空欄を埋めましょう。＞

1. INTRODUCTION

Purpose statement

The purpose of today's presentation is to compare JN Burger and Traditional Burger on three different points.

Objective statement

Hopefully, by the end of this presentation, you will better understand the similarities and differences between JN Burger and Traditional Burger and realize that _____ is the best choice.

2. BODY (At least 3 Topics)

Here are some tips for comparing (similarities) and contrasting (differencies).

Useful words and phrases

Compare

Similar, Like A, B is...,   Another similarity is...   Both A and B are...

Ex. Like shop A, shop B sells a set menu.

Another similarity is that both shop A and shop B are located near the station.

Contrast

> in contrast,　while,　Another difference is that…,　Unlike A , B is

Ex. · Shop A has more than twenty different hamburgers. In contrast, Shop B
　　　 has only five kinds of hamburgers.
　　　 · While Shop A has only thirty branches in Tokyo,　Shop B has fifty branches.

A. Topic 1: Similarities between JN Burger and Traditional Burger
<ヒント：まず、2つのお店の類似点を指摘します。>

	JN Burger	Traditional Burger
Capital Stock		
Number of Employees		
Number of Restaurants		

> **Topic sentence**
> I would like to talk about the similarities between JN Burger and Traditional
> Burger.

Supporting detail 1: Capital stock
<ヒント：下の空欄に説明文を書きましょう>

> JN Burger and Traditional Burger have a similar amount of capital.

DAY 5

Supporting detail 2: **number of employees**

<ヒント：下の空欄に説明文を書きましょう>

| |
| |

Supporting detail 3: **number of stores**

<ヒント：下の空欄に説明文を書きましょう>

| |
| |

Benefit for Topic 1

| |
| |

B. Topic 2: Differences in corporate profiles

<ヒント：Topic 2 と 3 では、2つのお店の異なる点を指摘します。>

	JN Burger	Traditional Burger
Motto		
Date of Establishment		
Uniqueness in Providing Ingredients		

Topic sentence

Next, we would like to take a look at some differences between JN Burger and Traditional Burger in their corporate profiles

Supporting detail 1: **Motto**

Supporting detail 2: **Date of establishment**

Supporting detail 3: **Uniqueness in providing ingredients**

Benefit for Topic 2

DAY 5

C. Topic 3: Menus

<ヒント：ホームページの情報を聞き手がわかりやすいようにまとめましょう。>

	JN Burger	Traditional Burger
Varieties of Hamburgers		
Prices of Hamburgers		
Varieties of Side Orders		

Topic sentence
Finally, we would like to compare their menus.

Supporting detail 1: **Varieties of hamburgers**

Supporting detail 2: **Prices of hamburgers**

Supporting detail 3: **Varieties of side orders**

Benefit for Topic 3

3. Conclusion

<ヒント：必要に応じて動詞の過去形を使いましょう>

	JN Burger	Traditional Burger
The similarities		
The differences		
Menus		

A. Purpose statement
B. Topic 1 and Benefit
C. Topic 2 and Benefit
D. Topic 3 and Benefit
E. Final remark (Objective statement)

DAY 6

Write a Presentation Script and Make a Poster

A Write a Script

TASK You've finished discussing your outline with your supervisor. Now you need to write the script. Based on the format used in Unit 1, write your presentation script, including a hook.

Your INTRODUCTION

Based on your outline, write your introduction.

Sample Introduction

Do you feel there aren't really so many differences among hamburger shops? Did you know that some hamburger shops have on-site vegetable production facilities? Or did you know that some hamburger shops import all their ingredients from the US to maintain their original taste? Thank you so much for giving us an opportunity to make a presentation on hamburger shops. My name is Utako Shimoda. And this is Hanako Suzuki. We are students at JW University. The purpose of today's presentation is to talk about JN Burger and Traditional Burger on three points: similarities in corporate profiles, differences in corporate profiles, and differences in menus. Hopefully, by the end of this presentation, you will clearly understand the similarities and differences between JN Burger and Traditional Burger.

Make a longer and more attractive hook

DAY 6

Your BODY

Based on your outline, write your body.

Topic 1

Sample Body

Topic 1

I would like to start by looking at the similarities between JN Burger and Traditional Burger. First, I would like to talk about capital. JN Burger has 3.5 billion yen in capital and Traditional Burger has 35 million dollars. They have about the same amount of capital. Another similarity is that both JN Burger and Traditional Burger have the same number of employees, 3,250. In addition, JN Burger and Traditional Burger have the same number of stores. As we have seen, JN Burger and Traditional Burger share the same amount of capital, and the same number of employees and stores.

We have talked about the similarities between JN Burger and Traditional Burger. What about the differences? Next I would like to talk about the differences, which we can find in the corporate profiles, of these two hamburger shops.

You can make a topic sentences with the following expressions:

To begin with ….
To start with ….
Let's start by looking at ….
I'd like to start by looking at ….
Let's start with…

Transition Paragraph

You need a transition paragraph to make a smooth change to the next topic.
The last sentence of a transition paragraph is the topic sentence of the next topic.

DAY 6

Topic 2

Topic 2

The first difference is about their mottos. The motto of JN Burger is "Sharing a wonderful and rich life with customers." In contrast, that of Traditional Burger is "Keep tradition and make history." We can see that JN Burger tries to keep up with its customers' needs, while Traditional Burger tries to keep their own tradition and style. Another difference is that Traditional Burger has a longer history than JN Burger. Traditional Burger was established in 1950, while JN Burger was established in 1975. There is another difference in the uniqueness of providing ingredients. Eighty percent of JN Burger stores have onsite vegetable production facilities to provide fresh food to customers. On the other hand, Traditional Burger makes efforts to serve products of the same quality, and they ship all the ingredients from their headquarters in the U.S. As you have seen, Traditional Burger has a longer history than JN Burger, and both have unique systems of ingredient distribution systems to realize their mottos.

I talked about the differences in their corporate profiles. What about their menus? Next I would like to talk about the differences in their menus.

DAY 6

Topic 3

Topic 3

The first difference in the menus is the variety of hamburgers. JN Burger has 5 different kinds, while Traditional Burger has just one kind. Another difference is the price of hamburgers. The average price of a hamburger at JN Burger is 276 yen. In contrast, the average price at Traditional Burger is 413 yen. The average price at JN burger is much lower than it is at Traditional Burger. We can also see differences in the varieties of side orders. JN Burger has more options than Traditional Burger. JN Burger has 6 options, whereas Traditional Burger has only 2. As you can see, JN Burger offers a greater variety of food at more reasonable prices, compared to Traditional Burger.

DAY 6

Your CONCLUSION

Based on your outline, write your conclusion.

Sample CONCLUSION

That concludes our presentation. Now, let us summarize the main points. First we explained the similarities between JN Burger and Traditional Burger. We talked about the capital, the number of employees and the number of stores, all of which are about the same between JN Burger and Traditional Burger. Second, we talked about the differences in their corporate profiles. We told you that Traditional Burger has a longer history than JN Burger, and that both have unique systems of food distribution to realize their own mottos. Finally, we compared their menus. We told you that JN Burger offers a greater variety of foods at more reasonable prices, compared to Traditional Burger. Hopefully, you have a better understanding of the similarities and differences between JN Burger and Traditional Burger. In terms of business success, the two companies are quite similar. However, for the customer, JN Burger is clearly the better choice. It offers more variety at lower prices. Thank you for listening. Do you have any questions?

DAY 6

Check Your Script

1. Does your script have at least five paragraphs?

      YES   NO

2. Is the purpose statement included in the INTRODUCTION?

      YES   NO

3. Is the objective statement included in the INTRODUCTION?

      YES   NO

4. Does each BODY paragraph have three supporting details?

      YES   NO

5. Does each BODY paragraph have a benefit statement?

      YES   NO

6. Does the CONCLUSION paragraph have three topic sentences and three benefits?

      YES   NO

7. Does the CONCLUSION paragraph repeat the objective statement?

      YES   NO

8. Did you use past tense or present perfect in the CONCLUSION paragraph?

      YES   NO

B Make a Poster

Based on the activity in Day 3 C, make a poster.

DAY 7
Rehearse Presentation

TASK   Your presentation is tomorrow. Now you practice your presentation with your friends.

Practice makes perfect. Find a partner and practice your presentation. Ask your partners to evaluate your presentation on the following points, rating each from 1 to 5.

1. **The speaker's voice was loud enough to hear.**

   1   2   3   4   5

   ↑ strongly disagree   ↑ strongly agree

2. **The delivery speed was appropriate.**

   1   2   3   4   5

3. **The speaker used the poster effectively.**

   1   2   3   4   5

4. **The speaker looked at the audience.**

   1   2   3   4   5

5. **You were interested in this presentation.**

   1   2   3   4   5

What questions would you like to ask the speaker?

_____

_____

_____

Final Task

Record your script into your cell phone and practice parallel reading until you can say all the words without looking at your script.

TASK You are going to have a job interview at an apparel company. The company has asked you to give a presentation in which you compare two apparel brands. Compare two fashion brands in Japan, and make a presentation.

<本ユニットの課題>
あなたは、ある企業の就職面接を受ける際に、その課題として日本のアパレル企業を２つ比較したプレゼンテーションを行うことになりました。日本のアパレル企業２つを比較してプレゼンテーションを行ってください。

JW Trend

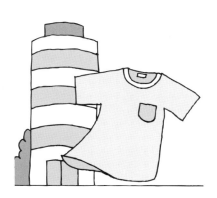

Traditional Cotton

DAY 8
Read an Article and Make an Outline

Ⓐ Read the article

You went to the career center for advice. The advisor suggested you read the following presentation before making an outline.

JW Trend and Traditional Cotton

Utako Shimoda

JW University

Did you know that JW Trend has more stores in Asia than Traditional Cotton? Do you think their annual sales are similar or different?

Thank you so much for giving me an opportunity to give this presentation. My name is Utako Shimoda, and I am a student at JW University. The purpose of today's presentation is to compare JW Trend and Traditional Cotton and to present some differences and similarities. By the end of this presentation, I hope you gain a better understanding of the similarities and differences between these two apparel companies.

1. Number of Stores

First I would like to talk about the number of stores. This is a bar graph that gives information on the number of stores for JW and TC. JW and TC have the same number of stores worldwide. Interestingly, both companies have the same number of stores in Japan, too. However, JW has a much smaller share in Europe than TC. TC has 150 stores in Europe, but JW has only 10. On the other hand, the number of JW stores in Asia is much greater than that of TC. JW has 150 stores in Asia, while TC has only 20. This graph shows that JW Trend is quite popular in Asia, while Traditional Cotton is popular in Europe.

We've talked about the number of stores. What about the ages of the customers? Are there any differences between JW Trend and Traditional Cotton? I would like to show you another graph to compare this point.

DAY 8

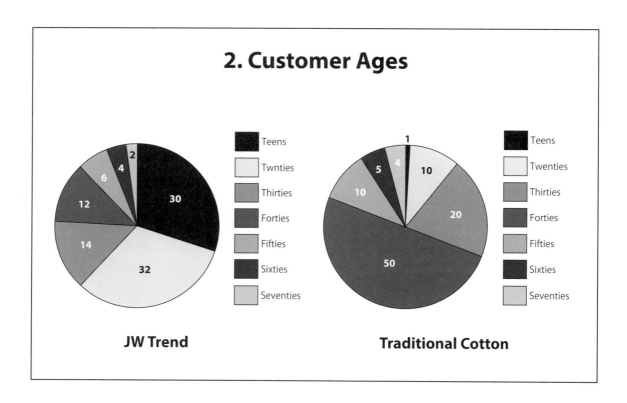

2. Customer Ages

JW Trend

Teens 30
Twnties 32
Thirties 14
Forties 12
Fifties 6
Sixties 4
Seventies 2

Traditional Cotton

Teens 1
Twenties 10
Thirties 20
Forties 50
Fifties 10
Sixties 5
Seventies 4

These two pie charts show the ages of JW Trend and TC customers. We can see that JW Trend is popular among people in their teens and twenties. About sixty percent of all the customers are in this age group. On the other hand, TC has the opposite trend. About seventy percent of customers are in their thirties and forties. It is less popular among teens and the elderly. To sum up, we can now say that JW is popular mainly among those in their teens and twenties, while TC is popular among those in their thirties and forties.

We've talked about the customers' ages. Now let's take a look at annual sales to see if there are any differences.

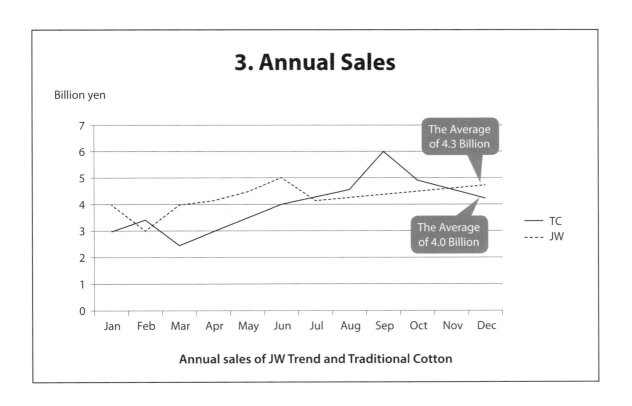

Annual sales of JW Trend and Traditional Cotton

I would like to compare the annual sales of JW Trend and Traditional Cotton using this line graph. Let's look at the dotted line, which shows the annual sales of JW. Sales in February plunged from 4 billion yen to about 3 billion. Then sales gradually increased from March to May, and peaked in June. However, sales in July dropped to about 4 billion yen and gradually increased toward December.

Now, let's take a look at TC. The solid line shows the annual sales of TC. Sales slightly increased from January to February but dropped to 2.5 billion yen in March. Then they gradually recovered and peaked in September at 6 billion. However, they had dropped drastically to about 4.8 billion by October and then gradually decreased to about 4 billion yen by December.

Finally, let's take a look at the annual sales average. JW had an average of 4.3 billion yen sales per month, while TC had 4.0 billion in sales per month. This graph shows that even though sales peaked in different months for JW Trend and Traditional Cotton, the overall sales trends are similar.

DAY 8

4. Conclusion

	JW Trend	**Traditional Cotton**
Popular in Region	Asia	Europe
Customers' Ages	Teens and Twenties	Thirties and Forties
Annual Sales	4.3 billion	4.0 billion

In conclusion, I'd like to summarize the main points. First I talked about the number of stores for JW Trend and Traditional Cotton. I told you that they have the same number of stores, and that JW is popular in Asia, while TC is popular in Europe. Second, I talked about the customers' ages. I told you that JW stores are popular among those in their teens and twenties, while TC stores are popular among those in their thirties and forties. Finally, I talked about annual sales. I told you that even though the companies had sales peaks in different months, the overall sales trends are similar for JW stores and TC stores. Hopefully, you now have a better picture of both companies. Thank you for listening. Do you have any questions?

B Describing a graph

Before you make an outline, let's learn how to describe graphs.

1. Types of graphs <ポイント：グラフの使い方を学習しましょう＞

Bar Graph

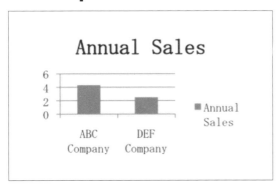

A bar graph is used to compare points between different groups. A bar graph is especially effective when the difference between the groups is large.

棒グラフは、グループ間の差異が大きいときに利用すると、効果的にその違いを示すことができます。

Line Graph

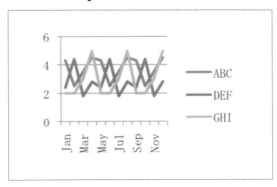

A line graph is used to track changes over short and long periods. A line graph is especially effective when the difference between the groups is small.

折れ線グラフは、短期あるいは長期間の変化を示したいときに有効です。グループ間の変化が少なくてもデータをわかりやすく提示できます。

Pie Chart

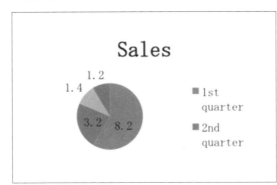

A pie chart is used to compare parts of a whole.

円グラフは全体を示しながら、その内訳を説明する際に有効です。

DAY 8

2. Describing graphs

Increased sharply

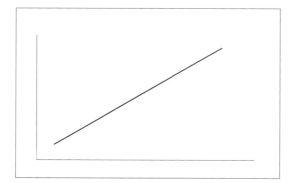

"Sales *increased sharply*."

Decreased sharply

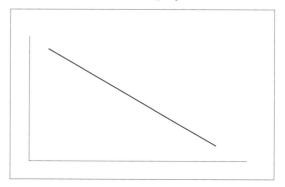

"Sales *decreased sharply*."

Increased gradually

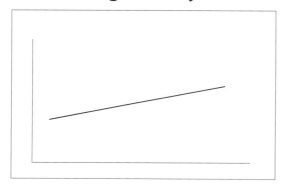

"Sales *gradually increased*."

Decreased gradually

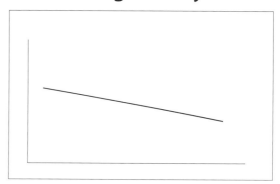

"Sales *gradually decreased*."

Peaked

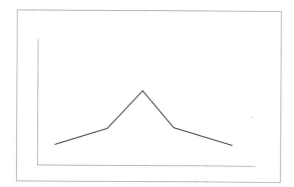

"Sales *peaked*."

Hit bottom

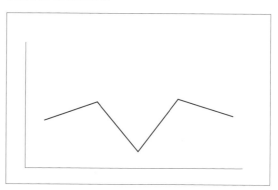

"Sales *hit bottom*."

Fluctuated

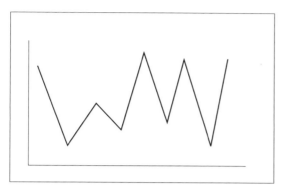

"Sales *fluctuated* throughout the whole year.

Kept Stable

"Sales *kept stable* for the whole year."

C Making an outline

Make your outline. Include graphs or charts in your presentation.

<ポイント：各トピックに表かグラフを使いましょう。>

1. INTRODUCTION

A. Hook <ポイント：聞き手を引きつけるための投げかけ>
B. Self-introduction
C. Purpose statement <ポイント：プレゼンテーションの目的>
D. Objective statement <ポイント：目標　このプレゼンテーションを聞いた後、聞き手にどうしてほしいのかの記述>

DAY 8

A. Topic 1: Number of Stores

1. Title: _____

Topic sentence

Description ＜表あるいはグラフの説明を先の例を参考に書きましょう＞

Benefit for Topic 1

B. Topic 2: Customer Ages

1. Title: _____

Topic sentence

Description ＜表あるいはグラフの説明を先の例を参考に書きましょう＞

Benefit for Topic 2

DAY 8

C. Topic 3: Annual Sales

1. Title: _____

Topic sentence

Description 〈表あるいはグラフの説明を先の例を参考に書きましょう〉

Benefit for Topic 3

3. CONCLUSION

A. Purpose statement

_____

B. Topic 1 and Benefit

_____

C. Topic 2 and Benefit

_____

D. Topic 3 and Benefit

_____

E. Final remark (Objective statement)

_____

DAY 9
Write a Presentation Script and Make a Poster

A Write a Script

TASK   You've finished discussing your outline with your supervisor. Now you need to write the script. Based on the format in Unit 1, write the script of your presentation with a hook.

Your INTRODUCTION

Based on your outline, write your introduction. Remember to include a hook in your introduction.

Your BODY

Based on your outline, write your body.

Topic 1

Topic 2

DAY 9

Topic 3

Your CONCLUSION

Based on your outline, write your conclusion.

Check Your Script

1. Does your script have at least five paragraphs?

    YES   NO

2. Is the purpose statement included in the INTRODUCTION?

    YES   NO

3. Is the objective statement included in the INTRODUCTION?

    YES   NO

4. Does each BODY paragraph have three supporting details?

    YES   NO

5. Does each BODY paragraph have a benefit statement?

    YES   NO

6. Does the CONCLUSION paragraph have three topic sentences and three benefits?

    YES   NO

7. Does the CONCLUSION paragraph repeat your objective statement?

    YES   NO

8. Did you use past tense or present perfect in the CONCLUSION paragraph?

    YES   NO

DAY 9

B Make a Poster

Based on the activity in Day 3 C, make a poster.

DAY 10
Rehearse Presentation

TASK   Practice with your friends. Your presentation is tomorrow!

Practice makes perfect. Find a partner and practice your presentation. Ask your partners to evaluate your presentation on the following points, rating each from 1 to 5.

1. **The speaker's voice was loud enough to hear.**

    1   2   3   4   5

    ↑ strongly disagree   ↑ strongly agree

2. **The delivery speed was appropriate.**

    1   2   3   4   5

3. **The speaker used the poster effectively.**

    1   2   3   4   5

4. **The speaker looked at the audience.**

    1   2   3   4   5

5. **You were interested in this presentation.**

    1   2   3   4   5

What questions would you like to ask the speaker?

_____

_____

_____

Final Task

Record your script into your cellphone and practice parallel reading until you can say all the words without looking at your script.

TASK As an employee of a large convenience store chain, you have been asked to make a product proposal, targeting convenience store customers. Write a proposal and give a presentation to the representatives of the manufacturing department.

<本ユニットの課題>
あなたは、ある製造会社で働いています。今回コンビニエンス・ストアで販売するための新しい商品開発の提案を依頼されました。企画書を書き、プレゼンテーションを企業の商品開発の担当者に行ってください。

DAY 11
Write a Product Proposal and Make an Outline

Ⓐ Write a product proposal.

商品の企画書を書いてみましょう。

Sample Proposal

Product Proposal

Product Name: *Fuwa Fuwa San*

ORIGINATOR: SHIMODA Utako   **DATE 2023 / 6 / 29**

OVERVIEW

Ice cream is one of the best-selling items in summer. And *Kari Kari Kun* has been one of the most popular brands of ice cream in Japan. The reasons are threefold. The first is price. The price is so reasonable that customers of all ages will not hesitate to purchase it. The second is flavor. Its soda flavor is so refreshing that it suits the needs of people who want to cool down. The third reason is simplicity. Due to its popsicle style, we can eat *Kari Kari Kun* anywhere, anytime without a spoon. We can open the package and eat it as soon as we buy it at a convenience store.

BACKGROUND AND OBJECTIVE

Kari Kari Kun is a very popular kind of popsicle among children and male adults. However, it is not so popular among young female adults. There are two reasons for this. First, since the popsicle melts much faster than ice cream in a cup, they cannot enjoy chatting with friends while eating it. Second, they much prefer Japanese-style ice cream such as vanilla with *azuki* and *shiratama*. However, since ice cream in a cup is quite expensive compared to *Kari Kari Kun*, its sales have been weak. This implies the need to develop a Japanese-style ice cream in a *Kari Kari Ku*n style. Such a product would likely sell very well. Therefore, I would like to propose a new product called *Fuwa Fuwa San*, which is a Japanese style ice cream bar at a reasonable price

PRODUCT DESCRIPTION

Fuwa Fuwa San is a Japanese-style ice cream bar. It has *azuki* and *shiratama* inside the vanilla ice cream so that people can enjoy the same taste of ice cream in a cup in a popsicle style. Also it doesn't melt for at least 10 minutes even in summer weather so people do not need to eat it in a rush.

TARGET

Women between 18 and 25 will be the target. The new package design will be developed to appeal to this target.

PRICE

60 yen (the same as *Kari Kari Kun*)

DAY 11

Product Proposal

Product Name: _____

ORIGINATOR: _____   DATE ___ / ___ / ___

OVERVIEW

BACKGROUND and OBJECTIVE

PRODUCT DESCRIPTION

TARGET

PRICE

B Make an outline

Write down your outline. You may use the ideas from the reading. Use phrases you learned in Unit 1.

Unit 1 で学習したフレーズを使ってアウトラインを書いてみましょう。

1. INTRODUCTION

A. Hook <ポイント：聞き手を引きつけるための投げかけ>
B. Self-introduction
C. Purpose statement <ポイント：プレゼンテーションの目的>
D. Objective statement <ポイント：目標　このプレゼンテーションを聞いた後、聞き手にどうしてほしいのかの記述>

2. BODY (3 Topics)

A. Topic 1: Overview

<ヒント：現在ある商品の利点について述べましょう>

Topic sentence
Supporting detail 1
Supporting detail 2
Supporting detail 3
Benefit

DAY 11

B. Topic 2: Background and Objective

<ヒント：現在ある商品の問題点とその解決策について述べましょう＞

Topic sentence	
Supporting detail 1	
Supporting detail 2	
Supporting detail 3	
Benefit	

C. Topic 3: Product description, Target and Price

Topic sentence	
Supporting detail 1	
Supporting detail 2	
Supporting detail 3	
Benefit	

3. CONCLUSION

<ヒント：必要に応じて動詞の過去形を使って表現しましょう>

A. Purpose statement
B. Topic sentence 1 and Benefit （Benefit を忘れずに）
C. Topic sentence 2 and Benefit （Benefit を忘れずに）
D. Topic sentence 3 and Benefit （Benefit を忘れずに）
E. Final remark (Objective statement)

DAY 12
Write a Presentation Script and Make a Poster

Ⓐ Write a Script

TASK You've finished discussing your outline. Now you need to write a script. Based on the format used in Unit 1, write the script for your presentation. Make sure to add a good hook to attract listeners to your presentation.

<ポイント：プレゼンテーションでは、イントロダクション hook を加えて、聞き手を引きつけるための工夫をします。Hook は日本語で言えば「釣り針」の意味で、「聞き手を釣り上げる」という比喩表現からこの言葉が使われるようになったようです。＞

Adding a Hook to the Introduction

A couple of interesting questions are often used as a hook.
<ポイント：hook は疑問文の形態をとることが多い。＞

\<Examples of a hooks>

● Don't you think ice cream in a cup is a little expensive?

● Have you ever wished for a popsicle that wouldn't melt so fast?

● Did you know that you can buy a popsicle that has *azuki* and *shiratama* in it?

Your INTRODUCTION

Based on your outline, write your introduction. Do not forget to add a hook.

Your BODY

Based on your outline, write your body.
The following signal words can be used in your script.

First, Second, Third,
For example, As another example, In addition,
Finally,
In conclusion,

Topic 1

DAY 12

Topic 2

Topic 3

Your CONCLUSION

Based on your outline, write your conclusion.

Check Your Script

1. Does your script have five paragraphs?

       YES   NO

2. Is a hook included in the INTRODUCTION?

       YES   NO

3. Is the purpose statement included in the INTRODUCTION?

       YES   NO

4. Is the objective statement included in the INTRODUCTION?

       YES   NO

5. Does each BODY paragraph have three supporting details?

       YES   NO

6. Does each BODY paragraph have a benefit statement?

       YES   NO

7. Does the CONCLUSION paragraph have three topic sentences and three benefits?

       YES   NO

8. Does the CONCLUSION paragraph repeat the objective statement?

       YES   NO

9. Did you use the past tense or present perfect in the CONCLUSION paragraph?

       YES   NO

DAY 12

B Make a Poster

Based on the activity in Day 3 C, make a poster.

DAY 13
Rehearse Presentation

TASK Your presentation is tomorrow. Now you practice your presentation with your friends.

Practice makes perfect. Find a partner and practice your presentation. Ask your partners to evaluate your presentation on the following points, rating each from 1 to 5.

1. **The speaker's voice was loud enough to hear.**

   1   2   3   4   5

   ↑ strongly disagree   ↑ strongly agree

2. **The delivery speed was appropriate.**

   1   2   3   4   5

3. **The speaker used the poster effectively.**

   1   2   3   4   5

4. **The speaker looked at the audience.**

   1   2   3   4   5

5. **You were interested in this presentation.**

   1   2   3   4   5

What questions would you like to ask the speaker?

_____

_____

_____

Final Task

Record your script into your cell phone and practice parallel reading until you can say all the words without looking at your script.

DAY 13

Self-evaluation Rubric II

以下の表中の①～③について、今の自分がどのレベルにいるか、それぞれあてはまるセルにチェックをしましょう。

	Level 1	Level 2	Level 3
① **Presentation Structure**	I can write an outline if I use this book. _____	I can write an outline without this book. _____	I can explain how to make an outline to my friends. _____
② **Presentation Script**	I can write a script if I have this book. _____	I can write a script without this book. _____	I can explain how to write a script to my friends. _____
③ **Presentation**	I can make a presentation if I have a script. _____	I can make a presentation without a script. _____	I can make an effective presentation using a poster. _____

TASK You've joined a presentation contest to be held at your university. Your topic will be "Is Study Abroad Necessary?" Prepare your presentation. You might want to carry out a small survey to obtain data.

<本ユニットの課題>
あなたは学内のプレゼンテーションコンテストに応募しました。テーマは「留学は必要か」で、発表時間は5分です。アンケートを行った結果もトピックの一つに含めましょう。

DAY 14
Read an Article and Make an Outline

Ⓐ Read the article

You've been assigned to read the following article in your English class. Read the article, and prepare for your presentation.

<ポイント：英語学習の重要性について次の英文を読んでみましょう。>

The Importance of Learning English

E111111
Utako Shimoda

Learning English or any other foreign language can be very challenging. You need to put a lot of effort into it. It is common to start a new foreign language, like German or Korean, when entering university, but please do not give up learning English. The reason is that you have already invested an enormous effort to improve your English. Even though you have been learning English for more than six years, many of you still think you cannot use the language as you expected. But you are almost there. If you try a little more, you will be able to speak English better!

DAY 14

The reason it takes time to improve English can be attributed to differences in linguistic structures between Japanese and English. Simply put, in Japanese sentences, the verb is usually at the end. On the other hand, in English sentences, the verb comes right after the subject. This difference makes it extremely hard for Japanese people to master English. In other words, it takes quite a lot of time for Japanese to get used to this difference. Even though learning English is difficult for us, we have to be aware that there are still some significant advantages to knowing English. This article discusses why we need to learn English and what kind of English we need to learn.

Why do we need to challenge ourselves to master English, one of the most difficult languages for Japanese people? The reason is quite simple. Being able to speak English is a powerful tool in today's global society. Did you know that about fifty percent of web pages all over the world are written in English? If we access only the web pages written in Japanese, we get only a little information on what is happening in the world. In other words, if we are able to read the pages in English, we can broaden our perspective much more. Second, it is very convenient if we can speak English when we go abroad. Nowadays, we can use English in almost all the countries of the world. Technically speaking, if we cannot speak English, we need to learn every language spoken in each country we visit. Now we can see how convenient it is if we can use English.

Furthermore, acquiring English gives us broader career opportunities. English is widely used as the language of business. Due to the advance of technology, we are required to process matters with speed. We cannot depend on translators or interpreters any more. We are expected to have meetings or exchange email with people overseas, who expect quick decisions in English. Many—even most—companies are looking for people who can communicate in English. Not only business but also the field of science requires researchers to have English communication skills since English is becoming the common language in academic settings.

Then what kind of English should we acquire? Do we all need native-like proficiency? The answer is "No." We do not need to be native speakers of English. What we need is the fluency in English to explain what is happening around us. Especially, in face-to-face communication, the skills to explain, to let people understand what we are trying to say, is very important. It is essential to maintain a positive attitude toward your English and to try to communicate to the best of your ability.

One of the goals to learn English used to be to reach native-like fluency, but not anymore. Past research findings on accents suggest the following three significant points regarding the level of fluency English learners should obtain. First of all, it is very rare for ESL or EFL learners to reach the level of native-like pronunciation. According to some research, only 2 to 3 % of learners can reach such a level. Second, a great deal of research suggests that learners of English communicate effectively even if their accents are different from those of native speakers. Third, some researchers claim that forcing learners to acquire native-like accents is a form of human discrimination since it can be seen as forcing learners to lose the identity associated with their first language. Based on this research, the idea of English as an International Language is gaining attention among researchers and policy makers.

English is often called an *international language* these days since it has been given an official status in so many countries. In Europe, they have their own framework called *CEFR, which is used worldwide, to describe language proficiency in reading, writing, speaking, and listening. In Southeast Asian countries such as Singapore and Malaysia, they have their own standards of English. The common idea behind these frameworks is that English is no longer a means to learn the cultures of the US, the UK, Canada, or Australia, where English is spoken as the first language. Rather it is simply a means of communication among people who do not share a first language.

In conclusion, this article has discussed the importance of learning English from three angles: first, the reason we need to learn English; second, what kind of English we need to learn; and third, how English is learned in other countries. In Japan, along with the introduction of the new Course of Study, all English teachers have to teach in English to promote communication in English not only with native speakers but also among people who do not share a first language. It is hoped that most Japanese people will feel more comfortable using English within several years.

*CEFR =Common European Framework of Reference for Languages

DAY 14

Summary

B Make a Survey.

Sample Survey Item

Thank you so much for contributing to my research. I will use the data obtained for research purposes only. Please answer the following questions.

1–Strongly disagree,   2–Disagree,   3–Neither agree nor disagree,
4–Agree,   5–Strongly agree

1. I want to study abroad
   1   2   3   4   5

2. I want to speak English better.
   1   2   3   4   5

3. I want to get a better job.
   1   2   3   4   5

4. I want to watch movies without subtitles.
   1   2   3   4   5

5. I want to get better scores on the TOEIC.
   1   2   3   4   5

6. I want to get married to a person from another country.
   1   2   3   4   5

7. I want to experience a homestay in another country.
   1   2   3   4   5

8. I want to work in another country in the future.
   1   2   3   4   5

9. I want to read English books without a dictionary.
   1   2   3   4   5

10. I want to exchange text messages with a person from another country.
   1   2   3   4   5

Thank you so much.

Sample Analysis of Survey

Item	1	2	3	4	5	6	7	8	9	10
Mean	2.5	2.5	2.7	4.3	3.5	2.1	3.4	3.5	2.3	3.4
SD	1.5	1.5	3.4	2.1	2.5	1.1	2.5	1.6	1.8	2.0

Mean = Average, **SD** = Standard Deviation

Analysis of Your Survey

Item	1	2	3	4	5	6	7	8	9	10
Mean										
SD										

Mean = Average, **SD** = Standard Deviation

C Making an outline

You would like to ask your supervisor some advice on your outline. First, make your outline. Include at least one graph or one chart in your presentation.

1. INTRODUCTION

A. Hook <ポイント：聞き手を引きつけるための投げかけ>
B. Self-introduction
C. Purpose statement <ポイント：プレゼンテーションの目的>
D. Objective statement <ポイント：目標　このプレゼンテーションを聞いた後、聞き手にどうしてほしいのかの記述>

2. BODY (At least 3 Topics)

A. Topic 1: Why we need to learn English

Topic sentence
Supporting detail 1
Supporting detail 2
Supporting detail 3
Benefit

B. Topic 2: What kind of English we need to learn: English as an International Language

Topic sentence
Supporting detail 1
Supporting detail 2
Supporting detail 3
Benefit

DAY 14

C. Topic 3: What are our thoughts on learning English?

1. Title: _____

Topic sentence

Description 〈表あるいはグラフの説明を先の例を参考に書きましょう〉

Benefit for Topic 3

3. CONCLUSION

A. Purpose statement

_____

B. Topic 1 and Benefit

_____

C. Topic 2 and Benefit

_____

D. Topic 3 and Benefit

_____

E. Final remark (Objective statement)

_____

DAY 15

Write a Presentation Script and Make a Poster

(A) Write a Script and Make a Poster

TASK You've finished talking with your supervisor. Now you can write your script.

Your INTRODUCTION

Based on your outline, write your introduction. Remember to include a hook in your introduction.

Your BODY

Based on your outline, write your body.

Topic 1

Topic 2

Topic 3

DAY 15

Your CONCLUSION

Based on your outline, write your conclusion.

Check Your Script

1. Does your script have at least five paragraphs?

    YES   NO

2. Is the purpose statement included in the INTRODUCTION?

    YES   NO

3. Is the objective statement included in the INTRODUCTION?

    YES   NO

4. Does each BODY paragraph have three supporting details?

    YES   NO

5. Does each BODY paragraph have a benefit statement?

    YES   NO

6. Does your BODY include at least one graph or one chart?

    YES   NO

7. Does the CONCLUSION paragraph have three topic sentences and three benefits?

    YES   NO

8. Does the CONCLUSION paragraph repeat the objective statement?

    YES   NO

9. Did you use the past tense or present perfect in the CONCLUSION paragraph?

    YES   NO

DAY 15

B Make a Poster

Based on the activity in Day 3 C, make a poster.

DAY 16
Rehearse Presentation

TASK   Practice with your friends. Your presentation is tomorrow!

Practice makes perfect. Find a partner and practice your presentation. Ask your partners to evaluate your presentation on the following points, rating each from 1 to 5.

1. **The speaker's voice was loud enough to hear.**

   1   2   3   4   5
   ↑ strongly disagree   ↑ strongly agree

2. **The delivery speed was appropriate.**

   1   2   3   4   5

3. **The speaker used the poster effectively.**

   1   2   3   4   5

4. **The speaker looked at the audience.**

   1   2   3   4   5

5. **You were interested in this presentation.**

   1   2   3   4   5

What questions would you like to ask the speaker?

_____

_____

_____

Final Task

Record your script into your cellphone and practice parallel reading until you can say all the words without looking at your script.

DAY 16

Self-evaluation Rubric III

以下の表中の①～③について、今の自分がどのレベルにいるか、それぞれあてはまるセルにチェックをしましょう。

	Level 1	Level 2	Level 3
① **Presentation Structure**	I can write an outline if I use this book. _____	I can write an outline without this book. _____	I can explain how to make an outline to my friends. _____
② **Presentation Script**	I can write a script if I have this book. _____	I can write a script without this book. _____	I can explain how to write a script to my friends. _____
③ **Presentation**	I can make a presentation if I have a script. _____	I can make a presentation without a script. _____	I can make an effective presentation using a poster. _____

Appendix

Sample Questions for Presentation

My name is Utako Shimoda. Thank you so much for your informative presentation. I would like to ask you a question regarding Topic 1.

- Could you explain your point again?
- What do you mean by $\sim$? Could you give us some examples?
- What is your opinion about the results of your survey?
- Where did the information in the chart come from?
- Why did you choose this data?
- When did you collect the data?
- Who were the participants in your survey?

Sample Compliments

- You spoke at a good pace.
- Your voice was very clear.
- Your poster was well organized.
- Your presentation was very informative.

Vocabulary

Unit 1

ambassador	大使
travel agencies	旅行代理店
location	場所
population	人口
climate	気候
attraction	アトラクション、名所
temperature	温度
accommodation	宿泊場所
cost	費用
approval	賛成
specific	特別な
confuse	困惑させる
objective statement	目標
purpose	目的
benefit	利益
tense	時制
opportunity	機会
unique	ユニークな
feature	特徴
hopefully	願わくは、期待して
bring in	連れてくる
tourists	観光客
degree	度
Celsius	摂氏
cherry blossom viewing	花見
autumn leaves	紅葉
various	様々な
high	高価な
medium	中くらいの
reasonable	安い
entertain	喜ばす

Unit 2

patronage	支援
serve	提供する
safe	安全な
motto	モットー
share with	～を分かちあう
tasty	おいしい

release	公表する
unique	独特な
burger	バーガー
curry	カレー
satisfy	満足させる
elderly	年配の方
challenge	挑戦する
catch up with	追いつく
product	製品
factory	工場
achieve	達成する
be equipped with	～が備わっている
on-site	施設内の
continue	続ける
apply	適応する
take orders	注文を取る
industry	産業
gain	増える
trust	信用
head office	本社
establishment	設立
capital	資本
fiscal year	会計年度
billion	10億
employee	従業員
operation	運営
introduce	紹介する
menu	メニュー
French fries	フライドポテト
soup	スープ
dessert	デザート
tradition	伝統
history	歴史、履歴
original	独自の
patty	パテ
quality	質
charcoal	炭
buns	バンズ
franchise	フランチャイズ
single	1つの
double	2つの

triple	3つの	bar graph	棒グラフ
root beer	ルートビア	especially	特に
similarity	類似点	effective	効果的な
in contrast	対照的に	sharply	鋭く
while	一方で	decrease	減少する
difference	違い	bottom	底
unlike	〜と異なって	fluctuate	上下に変動する
corporate profile	企業概要	stable	安定した
amount	量	audience	聴衆、聞き手

Unit 3

annual	年間の
apparel	アパレル
Europe	ヨーロッパ
popular	人気がある
show	示す
graph	グラフ
compare	比較する
age	年齢
customers	客
pie chart	円グラフ
trend	傾向
teens	10代
twenties	20代
share	シェア
middle age	中年層
to sum up	まとめると
thirties	30代
forties	40代
line graph	折れ線グラフ
plunge	急激に減る
gradually	徐々に
increase	増加する
drop	減る
peak	頂点
slightly	わずかに
recover	回復する
drastically	強烈に
average	平均
overall	全体を通して
region	地域
conclude	終わりにする
summarize	まとめる

Unit 4

purchase	購入する
product	製品
flavor	味、風味
popsicle	棒状のアイス
package	包み
vanilla	バニラ
taste	味
make haste	急ぐ

Unit 5

make an effort	努力する
enormous	大変な
improve	改善する
attribute	帰属する
linguistic	言語の
structure	構造
verb	動詞
subject	主語
extremely	非常に
master	マスターする
even though	〜にも関わらず
advantage	利益
article	記事
discuss	議論する
convenient	便利な
abroad	外国の
global	世界規模の
web pages	ホームページ
broaden	広げる
perspective	ものの見方
technically	技術的に

furthermore	さらに	significant	重要な、意味深い、（統計上）有意な
acquire	身につける		
broader	広い	following	次の
career	仕事上の、キャリア	regarding	〜に関して
opportunity	機会	rare	まれに
advance	先進	claim	主張する
technology	技術	force	無理に〜させる
require	要求する	discrimination	人種差別
process	処理する	identity	アイデンティティ
matters	案件	attention	注目、注意
translator	通訳者	policy maker	政策立案者
depend on	頼る	international language	国際語
exchange	交換する	official	公の
decision	決定	status	地位
company	企業	framework	枠組み
communicate	意思疎通を図る	worldwide	世界で幅広く
researcher	研究者	South East Asia	東南アジア
common language	共通語	standard	標準
academic	学術的な	means	手段
proficiency	熟達、プロフィシエンシー	angle	角度
		promote	促進する
positive	前向きな	comfortable	心地よい
attitude	態度	imagine	想像する
goal	目標	marry	結婚させる、結婚する
used to	かつては〜だった	efficient	効率的な
reach	届く	the United Nations	国際連合
level	水準	in addition	〜に加えて
fluency	流暢さ	in conclusion	結論的には
findings	わかった結果	parallel reading	パラレル・リーディング
accent	アクセント、発音	cell phone	携帯電話
suggest	提案する		

**実践プレゼンテーション・ワークブック
入門編（二訂版）**

検印 省略	©2017 年 1 月 31 日　第 1 版発行 2019 年 1 月 31 日　第 3 刷発行 2024 年 1 月 31 日　二訂版第 1 刷発行

編著者	中山　誠一 Jacob Schnickel Juergen Bulach
発行者	小川　洋一郎
発行所	株式会社 朝日出版社 101-0065　東京都千代田区西神田 3-3-5 電話（03）3239-0271 FAX（03）3239-0479 e-mail: text-e@asahipress.com 組版・Office haru ／製版・錦明印刷

乱丁、落丁本はお取り替えいたします
ISBN 978-4-255-15724-5 C1082

GLobal ENglish Testing System

大学生向け団体受験用テスト

CNN GLENTS Basic

グローバル英語力を測定
新時代のオンラインテスト

銀行のセミナー・研修でもお使いいただいています

Point 01
CNNの生の英語ニュースが素材

Point 02
場所を選ばず受験できるオンライン方式

Point 03
自動採点で結果をすぐに表示、
国際指標 CEFR にも対応

※画像はイメージです

期間限定キャンペーン実施中!

2,200 円（税込）で
テストが 2 回受けられます

英語力の定点測定に「CNN GLENTS Basic」を是非ご活用ください

受験人数	学生1名様からお申込みいただけます
受験期間	2023年4月1日（土）～ 2024年1月31日（水）

お試しいただいた先生の声

世界の出来事にアンテナを張り、深い教養や幅広い知識に磨きをかけることは、とても重要なことです。こうした普段からの意識的な努力が、CNN GLENTS Basicでは役に立ちます。一般社会において、仕事ができる人は、多少英語力が足りなくても、教養や知識で補って強引にでもコミュニケーションを成り立たせてしまう特徴があります。CNN GLENTSはこうした総合的な英語力を評価してくれると考えており、とても優れたテストだと思っています。

山中司先生 立命館大学
生命科学部生物工学科教授

立命館大学 生命科学部は、AI自動翻訳サービスを「プロジェクト発信型英語プログラム」の英語授業において 2022 年 9 月より試験導入するなど、常に新たな教育研究システムの開発に努めている学部です。

受験料：大学生 1 人あたり 2,200 円（税込）　受験料は、受けていただく学生の人数に応じてご相談させていただきます。

株式会社 朝日出版社「CNN GLENTS」事務局　☎0120-181-202　✉ glents_support@asahipress.com